Easter Bunny's Journey

Jane Quail

To order additional copies of this book, contact:
Xlibris Corporation
0-800-644-6988
www.xlibrispublishing.co.uk
orders@xlibrispublishing.co.uk

For Joshua

because he likes maps

Easter Bunny was feeling sad. He had one Easter egg left in his basket.

"What can I do now that Easter is over," he said.

After a while Easter Bunny went to sleep and he had a dream.

In his dream Easter Bunny spoke to a robin in her nest.

"Would you like an Easter egg?" he said.

"No thank you very much. I laid four eggs and now I have four chicks," she answered.

Easter Bunny dreamt that he went back 400 years in time and travelled to a country called France.

There he saw a dormouse who shook her head and cuddled her babies and didn't say anything.

Easter Bunny went back another 400 years and travelled on until he found a country called Italy.

"Would you like an Easter egg?" he asked an egret.

"No, no, no," she said.

Easter Bunny hurried away.

Easter Bunny travelled back another 400 years and reached a country called Greece.

He saw a stork who had built a nest on top of a very high pillar.

She called down to him, "I have two eggs hatching. Good-bye and have a safe journey."

Easter Bunny went back another 400 years and came to a country called Turkey.

There he met a wise owl who said, "Travel back another 400 years. If you see some camels follow them and if you see a star, go towards it."

Easter Bunny travelled back 400 years

AND

he saw a star

AND

he saw three camels.

Easter Bunny followed the camels until they came to a little house. The riders of the camels climbed down and each one gave a present to a little baby who lived in the house.

Easter Bunny didn't think that the presents looked very interesting. And then he had an idea.

"What about the last Easter egg in his basket?" he thought, so he crept inside and held the basket out to the baby. The baby smiled and clapped his hands.

Easter Bunny felt very happy and he started to run home. He could run quickly now that he didn't have a basket to carry anymore and so he was soon back.

AND THEN HE WOKE UP.

THE END

And the beginning.

Because Easter Bunny is collecting eggs for next Easter now.

He has bought a new Basket to put them in.

TURKEY

ISRAEL

CPSIA information can be obtained
at www.ICGtesting.com
Printed in the USA
LVIW010702200812

2979LVUK00002B